15 Romantic Pieces for Flute and Piano

Transcribed by Paula Robison

ED 4173

ISBN 978-0-634-06219-3

G. SCHIRMER, *Inc.*

7777 W. BLUEMOUND RD. P.O. BOX 13819 MILWAUKEE, WI 53213

Visit us Online:
www.schirmer.com
www.halleonard.com

Paula Robison comes from a family of writers, actors, dancers, and musicians. A graduate of The Juilliard School, she gave her New York recital debut under the auspices of Young Concert Artists and the next year became the first American to win First Prize in flute at the Geneva International Competition. When the Chamber Music Society of Lincoln Center was formed, Ms. Robison was invited to be a founding member. She performed with the Society for twenty years. During the same period she was co-director, with Scott Nickrenz, of the Concerti di Mezzogiorno at the Spoleto Festival, winning the Adelaide Ristori Prize for her contribution to Italian cultural life.

Paula Robison has commissioned concertos for flute and orchestra by Leon Kirchner, Toru Takemitsu, Robert Beaser, Oliver Knussen, and Kenneth Frazelle. She gives master classes and woodwind performance seminars all over the world.

Contents

Foreword

As I think about my life as a solo flutist I especially treasure the wonderful pianists with whom I've had the joy of performing, and the lasting friendships which have been the gift of our collaborations.

Each of the transcriptions in this collection was inspired by a particular artist: Ruth Laredo and her expansive Rachmaninoff; Timothy Hester's wit and daring; Jeremy Denk's searching mind; Richard Goode's poetry; Yefrim Bronfman's laughter; Samuel Sander's loving camaraderie; Kenneth Cooper's adventures; Patricia Zander's elegant Fauré; Jean-Yves Thibaudet's masterful illumination of Edvard Grieg; and Charles Wadsworth's tender "To a Wild Rose." I thank each of these artists with all my heart.

This book is dedicated to the idea that we flutists have always been singers and storytellers and that we possess the gift to describe with our instruments the most beautiful mysteries of life.

Of the fifteen works included in this collection, four are instrumental in origin. The rest are songs. I include paraphrases of the original texts as a pathway to their meaning. May this music enrich your life as much as it has mine.

Paula Robison
New York City
July 2003

Song Texts

Love Song (Chanson d'amour)
poem by Armand Silvestre music by Gabriel Fauré

I love your eyes, your face, your lips where my kisses burn, oh my rebellious one! I love everything that makes you beautiful... from your head to your feet...

After a Dream (Après un rêve)
poem by Romain Bussine music by Gabriel Fauré

I slumbered–your image enchanted my dreams—you called to me–you were radiant and kind. The divine heavens opened for us. We rose together towards the light... Alas! Sad awakenings! Oh, night, bring back your illusions... Return, mysterious night...

Gentle Annie
words by Stephen Foster music by Stephen Foster

Thou wilt come no more, gentle Annie—Like a flower thy spirit did depart—Thou art gone, alas! Like the many that have bloomed in the summer of my heart...

Beautiful Dreamer
words by Stephen Foster music by Stephen Foster

Beautiful dreamer, wake unto me—Starlight and dew drops are wanting for thee... Sounds of the rude world heard in the day, lulled by the moonlight have all passed away! Beautiful dreamer, queen of my song, beam on my heart! Awake unto me!

I Love You! (Jeg elsker Dig!)
words by Hans Christian Andersen music by Edvard Grieg

A joyous and passionate declaration of eternal love.

Two Brown Eyes (To brune Øjne)
words by Hans Christian Andersen music by Edvard Grieg

A husband sings to his wife of her sweet eyes and how his whole world lives within them.

Solveig's Song (Solveigs Sang)
words by Henrik Ibsen — music by Edvard Grieg

Solvieg sits in the sun at her doorway and sings of her wandering lover Peer Gynt, sure that they will be reunited even if it is after death.

The Birds (Die Vögel)
poem by Karl Wilhelm Friedrich von Schlegel — music by Franz Schubert

How delightful it is to glide and sing high in the sky—to look down on the poor humans moaning about their troubles; they can't fly like we can!

Night and Dreams (Nacht und Träume)
poem by Matthäus von Collin — music by Franz Schubert

Blessed night—you float down, filled with dreams and moonlight, into our quiet hearts. Holy night, come to us!

To Music (An die Musik)
poem by Franz von Schober — music by Franz Schubert

A hymn of Thanksgiving to the gracious Art which, in our grey hours, when we're surrounded by the fiercest circles of life, rescues us and fills our hearts with Love and the knowledge of a better world. Music, we thank you.

Night (Die Nacht)
poem by Hermann Gilm — music by Richard Strauss

The night steps softly out of the forest, surrounding us, taking away all the flowers and colors of the world... come close to me; I fear it will take you away from me too.

CHANSON D'AMOUR
(Love Song)

Gabriel Fauré
Op. 27, No. 1
Arr. by Paula Robison

16
cresc.
cresc.
20
f
espr.
p dolce
mf
p
24
mp
p
pp sub.
p
pp sub.
28
senza rigore
a tempo
mf
p
marcato
31
p dolcissimo
p

35
cresc. poco a poco
mf
cresc. poco a poco
mf
39
p léger, ardent
pp
43
mp
pp
47
poco rit.
a tempo
dolciss.
marcato
51

APRÈS UN RÊVE
(After a Dream)

Gabriel Fauré
Op. 7, No. 1
Arr. by Paula Robison

17
mf
f espr.
f cantando
mf
mf

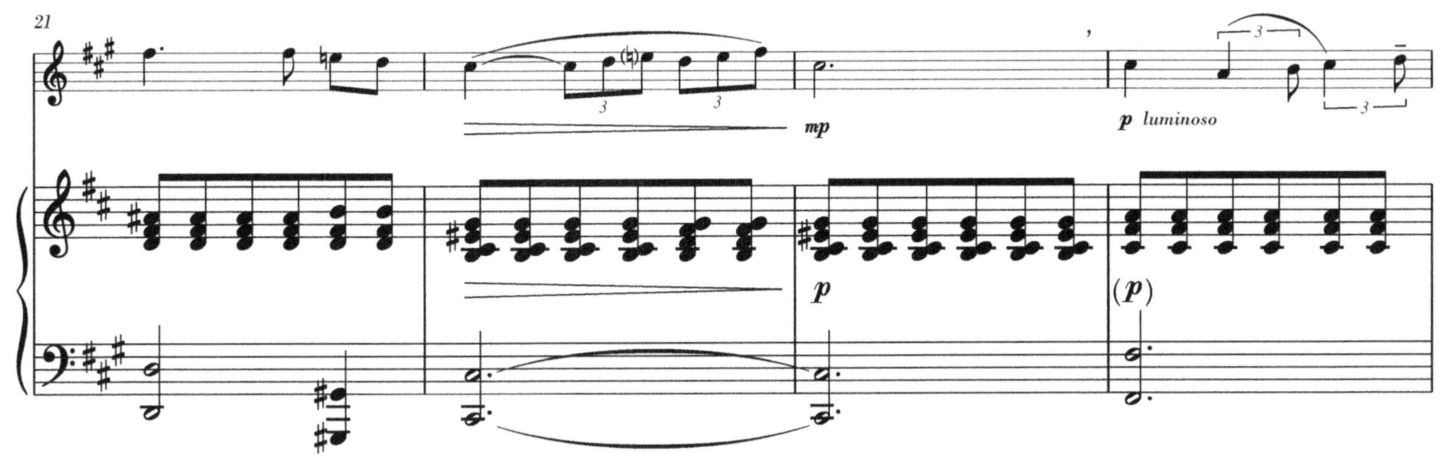
21
mp
p luminoso
p
(p)

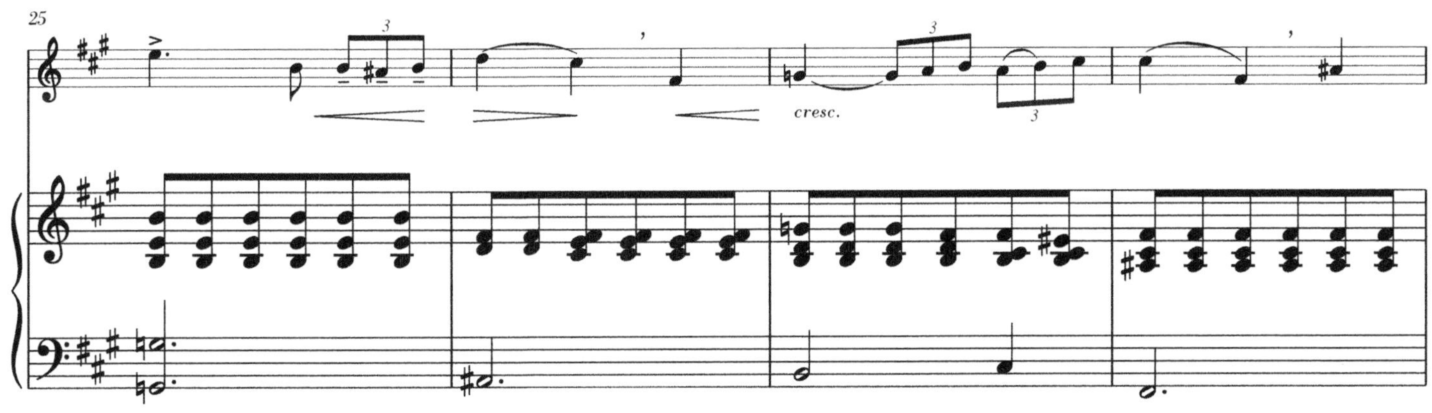
25
cresc.

29
più cresc.
f molto espressivo
f
dim.

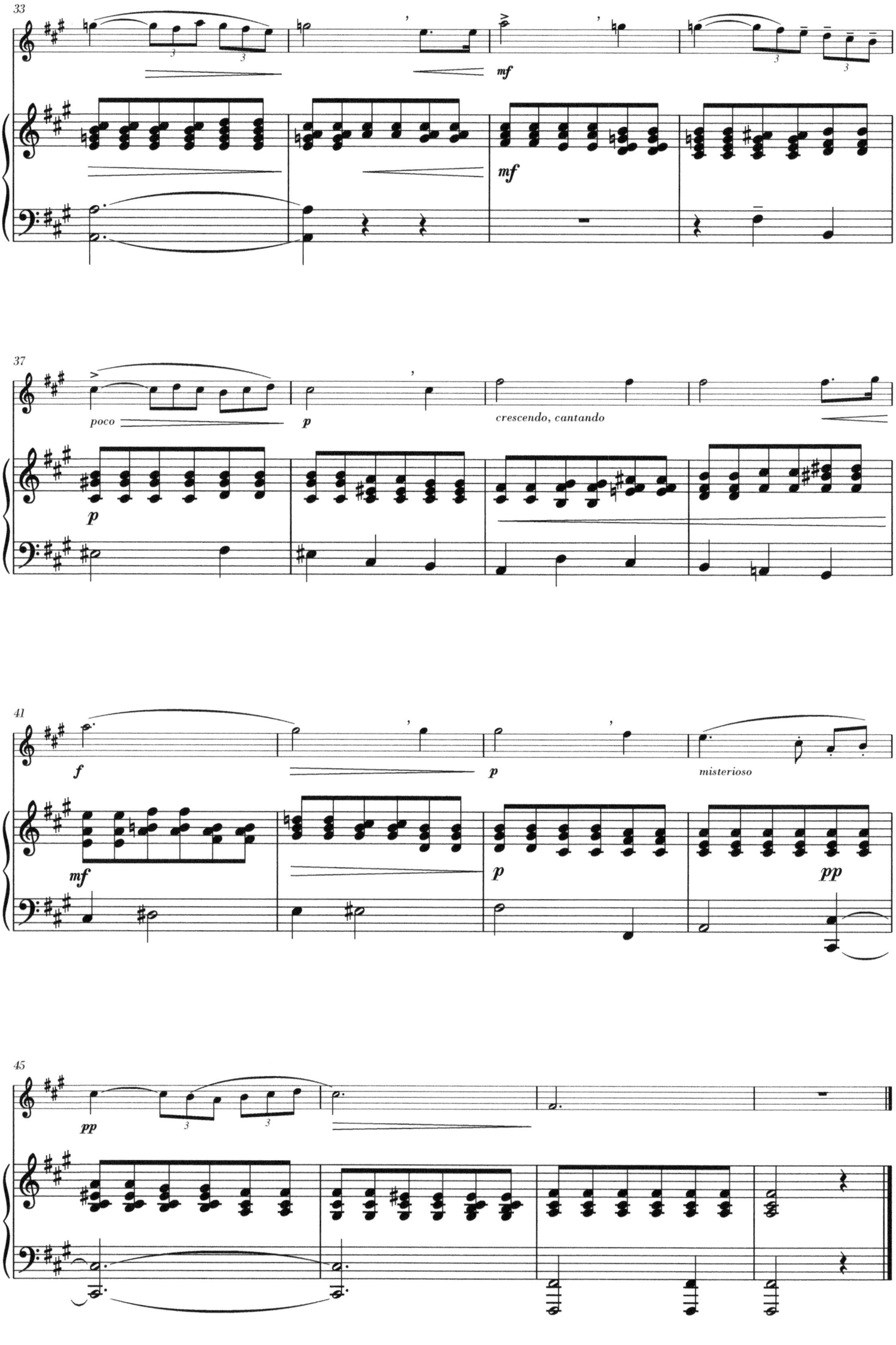

33

mf

mf

37

poco

p

crescendo, cantando

p

41

f

mf

p

misterioso

p

pp

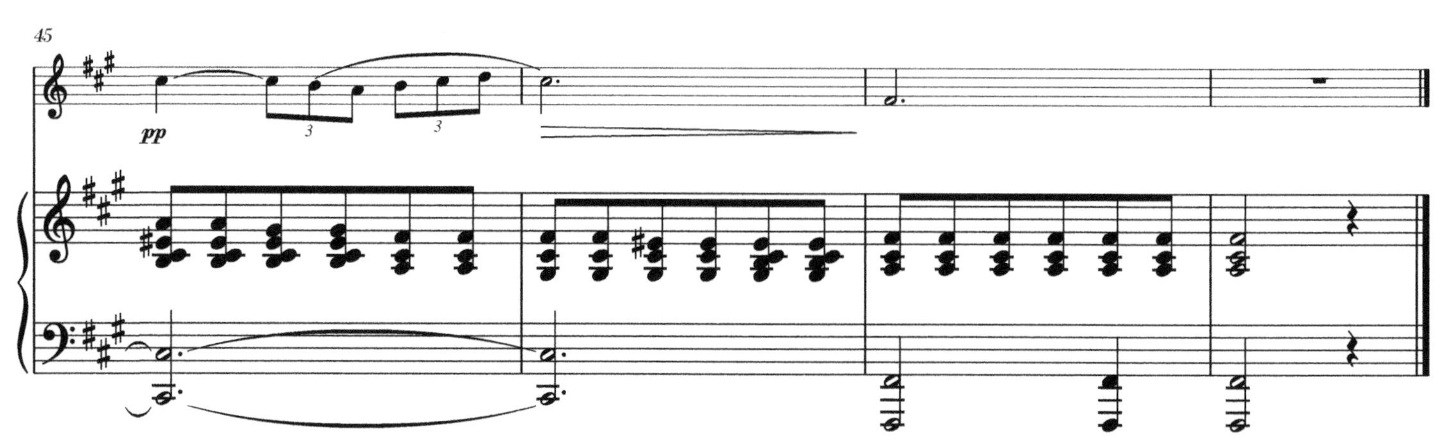

JENNIE'S OWN SCHOTTISCH
from *The Social Orchestra*

Stephen Foster
Arr. by Paula Robison

19
dolce
dolce

a tempo
24
p
flirtatious
p

1
29

2
poco ritard
33
p delicato
pp delicato

38
f
f
43
48
poco rit.
a tempo
mf grazioso
mf
53
rit.
dim.
p
grazioso
dim.
p

GENTLE ANNIE

Stephen Foster
Arr. by Paula Robison

13
mf
espr.
16
mp
mp
19
mf
22
3
pp
25
pp

28
31
pp dolciss.
pp
34
(pp)
pp
38
rall.
a tempo
dolciss.
dolce
41
dolce

BEAUTIFUL DREAMER

Stephen Foster
Arr. by Paula Robison

14
cresc.
17
mf
mf
20
rall.
a tempo
cresc.
p
p
ad lib.
24
f cantando
mf
28
espr.

31
34
broaden
p sub. dolce, ardente
p
cresc.
cresc.
37
a tempo
f
f
40
rall.
mf
f gioioso, ardente
ad lib.
43
a tempo
dolce
rall.

JEG ELSKER DIG!
(I Love You!)

Edvard Grieg
Op. 5, No. 3
Arr. by Paula Robison

11
poco accel.
poco a poco cresc.
14
sempre cresc.
Ped.
16
rit.
f
ff
molto espressivo, gioioso
f
ff
p
Ped.
Ped.
Ped.
19
dim., in tempo
pp

TO BRUNE ØJNE
(Two Brown Eyes)

Edvard Grieg
Op. 23, No. 19
Arr. by Paula Robison

14
a tempo
poco tenuto
poco tenuto
a tempo
17
p
20
poco rit.
espr.
23
dolce
pp

BRYLLUPSDAG PÅ TROLDHAUGEN

(Wedding Day at Troldhaugen)

from *Lyric Pieces* for Piano

Edvard Grieg
Op. 65, No. 6
Arr. by Paula Robison

Troldhaugen is the site of the composer's country villa.
This piece was written as an anniversary gift to his wife.

17
sempre pp
21
f
p dolce
dim.
pp dolce
una corda
25
tre corde
28
dim.
pp
una corda
pp sempre
sempre
32
pp sempre
simile

34
tr
Ped.
tre corde
36
cresc.
poco a poco
Ped.
38
tr
più cresc.
più cresc.
Ped.
40
f
f
Ped.
42
Ped.

Flute

TO A WILD ROSE

15 Romantic Pieces for Flute and Piano

Transcribed by Paula Robison

Contents

ED 4173

G. SCHIRMER, *Inc.*

7777 W. BLUEMOUND RD. P.O. BOX 13819 MILWAUKEE, WI 53213

Flute

CHANSON D'AMOUR
(Love Song)

Gabriel Fauré
Op. 27, No. 1
Arr. by Paula Robison

Flute

APRÈS UN RÊVE
(After a Dream)

Gabriel Fauré
Op. 7 No. 1
Arr. by Paula Robison

Flute

JENNIE'S OWN SCHOTTISCH

from *The Social Orchestra*

Stephen Foster
Arr. by Paula Robison

27
30
1
2
poco ritard
33
p delicato
37
40
3
f
43
tr
tr
tr
47
tr
tr
poco rit.
a tempo
mf grazioso
51
54
rit.
dim.
p
grazioso

Flute

GENTLE ANNIE

Stephen Foster
Arr. by Paula Robison

Flute

BEAUTIFUL DREAMER

Stephen Foster
Arr. by Paula Robison

Flute

JEG ELSKER DIG!
(I Love You!)

Edvard Grieg
Op. 5, No. 3
Arr. by Paula Robison

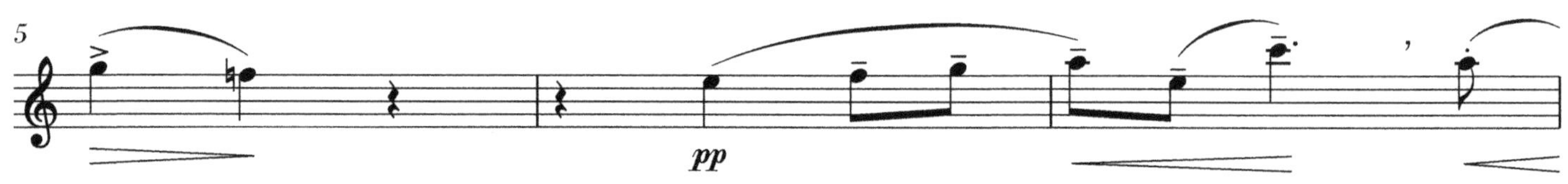

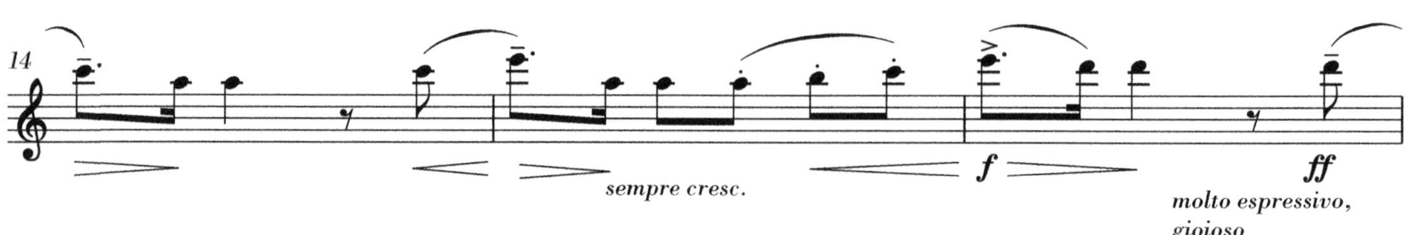

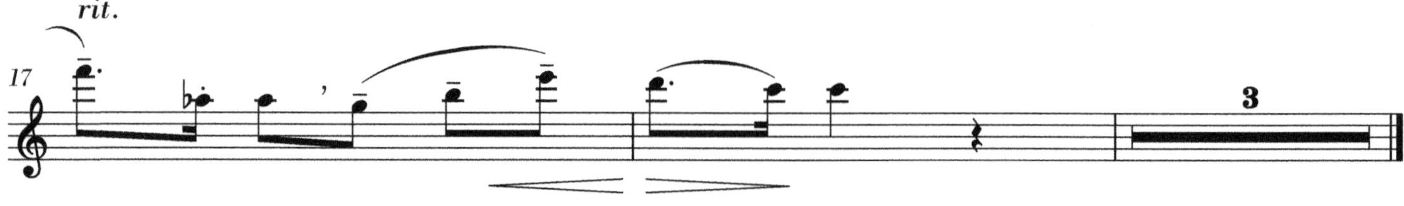

Flute

TO BRUNE ØJNE
(Two Brown Eyes)

Edvard Grieg
Op. 65, No. 6
Arr. by Paula Robison

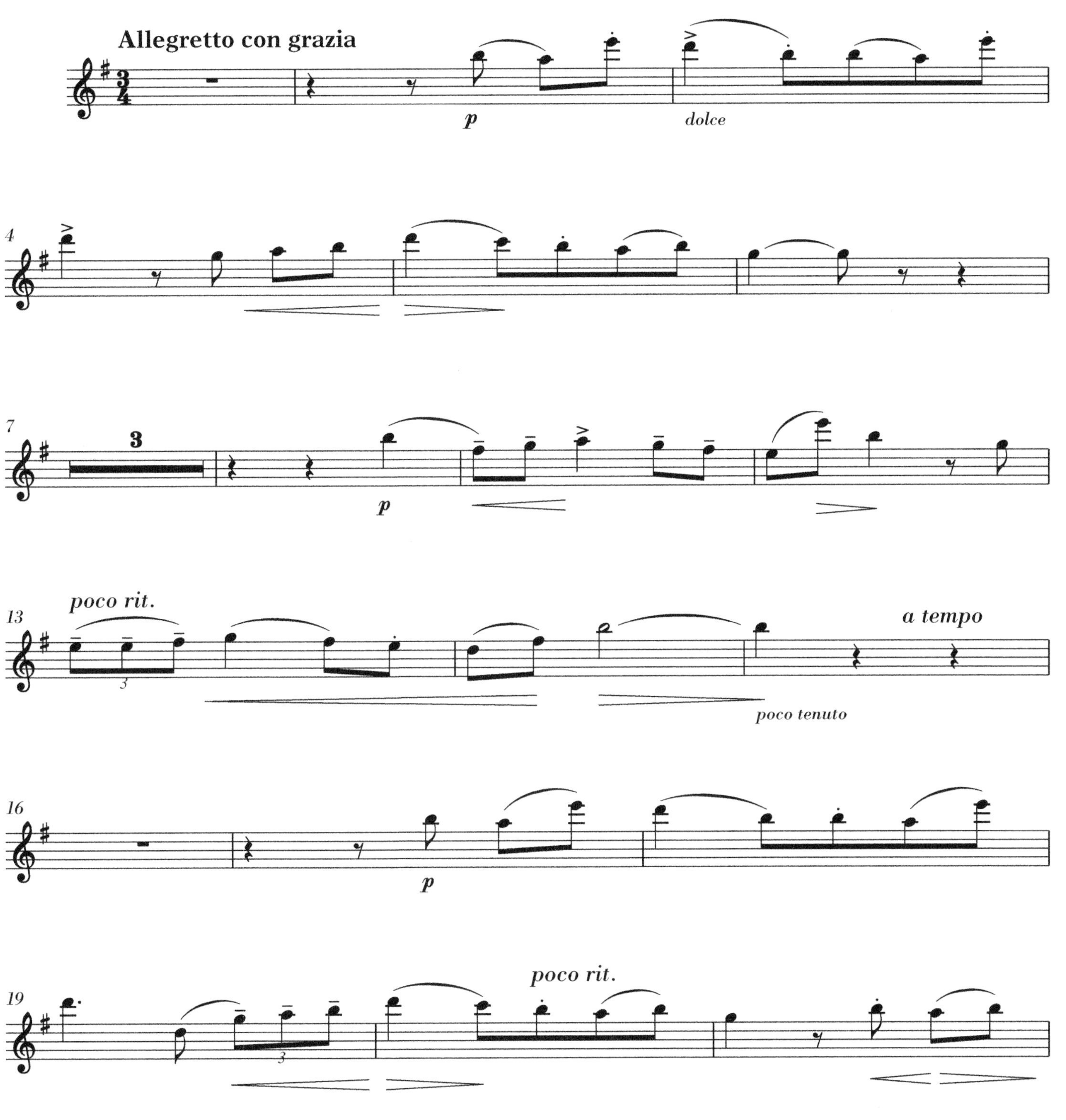

Flute

SOLVEIGS SANG
(Solveig's Song)
from *Peer Gynt*

Edvard Grieg
Op. 23, No. 19
Arr. by Paula Robison

Tempo I
pp
p darker
mf
poco animato
poco rit.
a tempo
mf
f
poco sost.
rit.
p
Allegretto con moto
pp
con una dolce speranza
espr.
Tempo I

Flute

BRYLLUPSDAG PÅ TROLDHAUGEN
(Wedding Day at Troldhaugen)
from *Lyric Pieces* for Piano

Edward Grieg
Op. 65, No. 6
Arr. by Paula Robison

Tempo di marcia un poco vivace

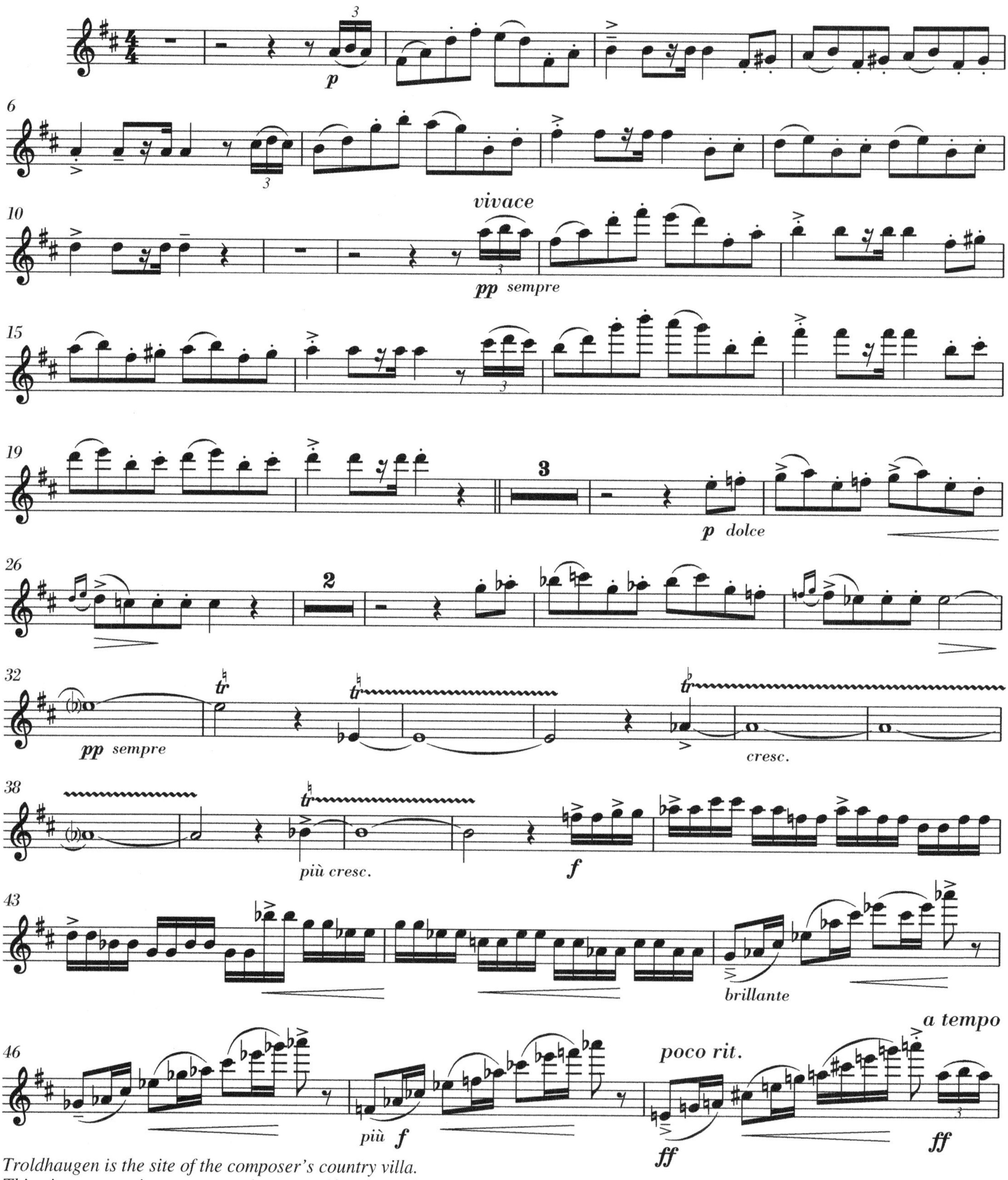
p
vivace
pp sempre
p dolce
pp sempre
cresc.
più cresc.
f
brillante
più f
poco rit.
a tempo
ff
ff

Troldhaugen is the site of the composer's country villa. This piece was written as an anniversary gift to his wife.

49
fz
fz
fz
3
53
fz
fz
57
Poco tranquillo
18
75
dolce cantando
pp dolciss.
84
p warmly
94
f
104
Tempo I
espr.
3
3
p
110
3
114
vivace
3
pp dolce
119
3
123
3

130
pp dolce
p
136
pp
pp sempre
141
cresc.
più cresc.
147
f
150
f
152
ff
154
gioioso
ff
fff
157
fz
f
161
ff sempre
mp
167
174
pp like bells
pure bell sound
dim.
ffz

Flute

TO A WILD ROSE
from *Woodland Sketches*

Edward MacDowell
Op. 51
Arr. by Paula Robison

Flute

PRELUDE IN G MAJOR

Sergei Rachmaninoff
Op. 32, No. 5
Arr. by Paula Robison

Flute

NACHT UND TRÄUME
(Night and Dreams)

Franz Schubert
Op. 43, No. 2
Arr. by Paula Robison

Flute

DIE VÖGEL
(The Birds)

Franz Schubert
Op. 172, No. 6
Arr. by Paula Robison

Flute

AN DIE MUSIK
(To Music)

Franz Schubert
Op. 88, No. 4
Arr. by Paula Robison

Flute

DIE NACHT
(Night)

Richard Strauss
Op. 10, No. 3
Arr. by Paula Robison

44
brillante
più f
marc.
più f
48
poco rit.
a tempo
ff
ff
fz
fz
51
fz
fz
54
fz
fz
fz
fz

Poco tranquillo
p
cantando
f
dolce cantando
pp dolce
una corda
pp dolciss.
pp dolce

87
p warmly
p
92
97
f
f
tre corde
102
espr.
107
Tempo I
p
p

111
115
vivace
pp dolce
pp
una corda
119
sempre pp
123
127
f
tre corde
dim.
pp dolce
una corda

131
f
tre corde
Ped.
134
p
pp sub.
dim.
pp
pp sempre
una corda
sempre
138
pp sempre
simile
140
cresc.
142

144
tr
più cresc.
più cresc.
Ped.
146
f
f
Ped.
148
Ped.
150
6
5
5
f
ff
marc.
Ped.
Ped.

153
gioioso
ff
più f
poco rit.
a tempo
155
fff
ff
158
fz
fz
161
tr
ff sempre
ff sempre
staccato sempre

164
166
mp
p
168
170
dim
174
pp like bells
pure bell sound
dim.
ffz
pp sopra
pp
ffz
una corda

SOLVEIGS SANG
(Solveig's Song)

from *Peer Gynt*

Edvard Grieg
Op. 23, No. 19
Arr. by Paula Robison

a tempo
pp
f
p
Allegretto con moto, lilting
pp una corde
sempre
Tempo I
pp
p darker
p darker
mf

50
poco animato
poco rit.
a tempo
poco sost.
mf
f
f
55
rit.
Allegretto con moto
p
pp
con una dolce speranza
p
pp
una corde
Ped.
Ped.
sempre Ped.
61
espr.
67
Tempo I
3
pp
72
p
dim.
pp

TO A WILD ROSE
from *Woodland Sketches*

Edward MacDowell
Op. 51
Arr. by Paula Robison

With simple tenderness ♩ = 88

24 rit.
cresc. f dimin. mp pp
cresc. f dimin. mp pp

29
p p
p p

35 accompagnando
espr.

41
mp p espr.
mp p

46 poco rit. a tempo
pp dolce ppp
pp dolce ppp

PRELUDE IN G MAJOR

Sergei Rachmaninoff
Op. 32, No. 5
Arr. by Paula Robison

9
ppp
pp
ppp
p
11
13
dim.
pp dolce,
leggiero
pp
15
dim.

17
p
p
19
pp
pp
21
tr
23
tr
f
tr
perdendo
mf dolce

25
pp
p
pp
27
p
rit.
a tempo
p luminous
pp dim.
29
31

33
3
3
pp
p
3
5
5
5
5
5
5
5
6
35
p leggiero
pp leggiero
5
5
5
5
5
5
5
5
37
p
perdendo
p
perdendo
5
5
5
5
5
5
39
tr
pp
dolciss.
pp dolciss.
5
5
5
5

NACHT UND TRÄUME
(Night and Dreams)

Franz Schubert
Op. 43, No. 2
Arr. by Paula Robison

9
11
13
dolciss.
15
pp
cresc.
ppp
17
luminous

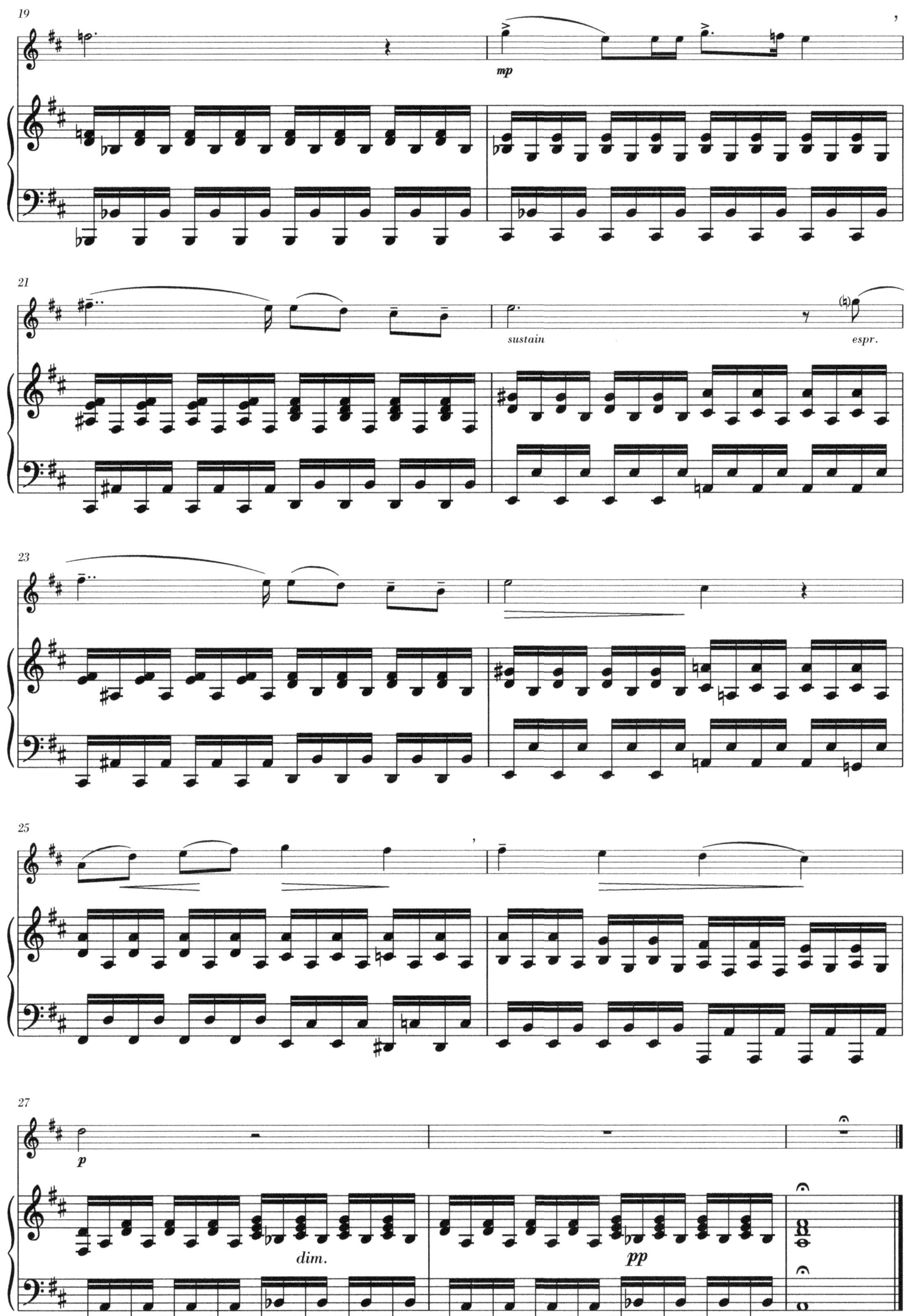
19
mp
21
sustain
espr.
23
25
27
p
dim.
pp

DIE VÖGEL
(The Birds)

Franz Schubert
Op. 172, No. 6
Arr. by Paula Robison

28
mp
pp
34
grazioso
grazioso
39
mf
espr.
44
p
pp
mp
49
delicato, volando

AN DIE MUSIK
(To Music)

Franz Schubert
Op. 88, No. 4
Arr. by Paula Robison

20
fp
fp
pp dolce
pp
dolce espr.
25
dolcissimo
30
dolce espr.
34
cresc.
cresc.
p
dolce
39
fp
fp

DIE NACHT
(Night)

Richard Strauss
Op. 10, No. 3
Arr. by Paula Robison

15
espr.
darker
pp
pp
Ped.
19
cresc.
più cresc.
sempre pp
sempre pp
23
p espr.
dim.
Ped.
Ped.
Ped.
27
p
cresc.
pp

30

mf *mf*

cresc.

Ped. ❇ Ped. ❇ Ped. ❇

34

mp dim. *p dolce*

Ped. ❇ Ped. ❇ Ped. ❇ Ped. ❇

38

dolciss. espr. *pp*

cresc. *pp espr.* *sf*

Ped. ❇ Ped. ❇

42